RHYMES AROUND THE DAY

For Laura

KESTREL BOOKS
Published by Penguin Books Ltd
Harmondsworth, Middlesex, England

This selection copyright © 1983 by Pat Thomson
Illustrations copyright © 1983 by Jan Ormerod

First published 1983

ISBN 0 7226 5808 7
Printed in Great Britain by William Clowes (Beccles) Ltd

Jan Ormerod

RHYMES
AROUND
THE DAY

Chosen by Pat Thomson

KESTREL BOOKS

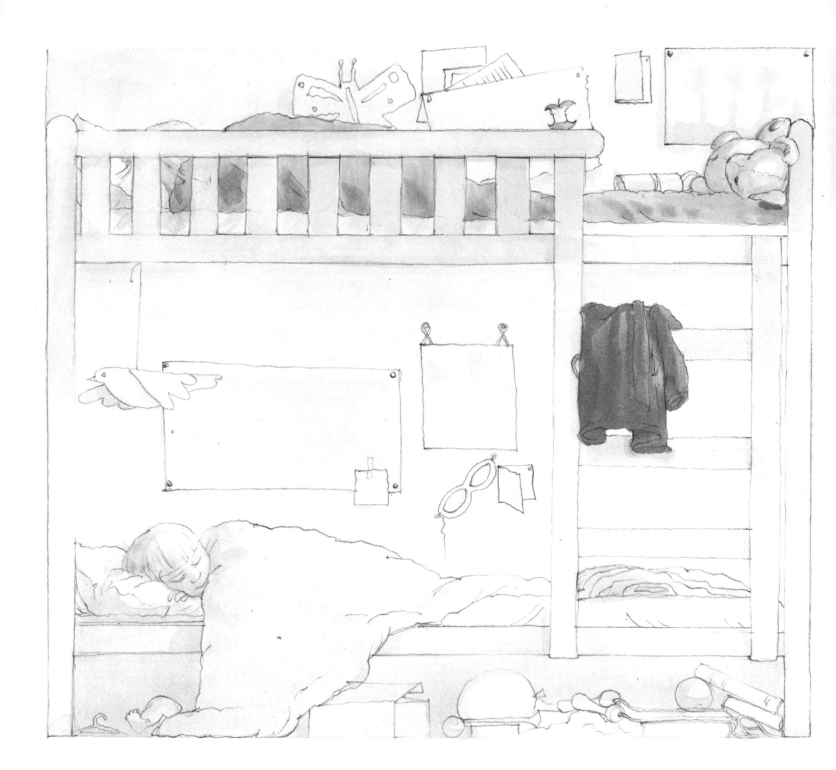

The cock does crow
To let you know
If you be wise
'Tis time to rise;
For early to bed
And early to rise,
Is the way to be healthy
And wealthy and wise.

I can tie my shoelaces,
I can brush my hair,
I can wash my face and hands
And dry myself with care.
I can clean my teeth, too,
Fasten up my frocks,
I can dress all by myself
And pull up both my socks.

Humpty Dumpty sat on a wall,
Humpty Dumpty had a great fall;
All the King's horses
And all the King's men
Couldn't put Humpty Dumpty together again.

Can you walk on tiptoe
As softly as a cat?
Can you stamp along the road
Stamp, stamp, just like that?
Can you take some great big strides
Just like a giant can?
Or walk along so slowly,
Like a bent old man?

Smiling girls, rosy boys,
Come and buy my little toys,
Monkeys made of gingerbread
And sugar horses painted red.

When Jacky's a good boy,
He shall have cakes and custard;
But when he does nothing but cry
He shall have nothing but mustard.

Handy pandy, Jack-a-dandy,
Went to buy some sugar candy.
He bought some at the corner shop,
And out he came with a hop, hop, hop!

One-ery, two-ery, dickery dan,
Choose the right hand if you can!

To market, to market
To buy a plum bun.
Home again, home again,
Market is done.

Diddle, diddle, dumpling,
My son John,
Went to bed with his trousers on.
One shoe off, and the other shoe on,
Diddle, diddle, dumpling,
My son John.

One, two,
Buckle my shoe;
Three, four,
Knock at the door;
Five, six,
Pick up sticks;
Seven, eight,
Lay them straight;
Nine, ten,
A big fat hen.

Eleven, twelve,
Dig and delve;
Thirteen, fourteen,
Maids a-courting;
Fifteen, sixteen,
Maids in the kitchen;
Seventeen, eighteen,
Maids in waiting;
Nineteen, twenty,
My plate's empty.

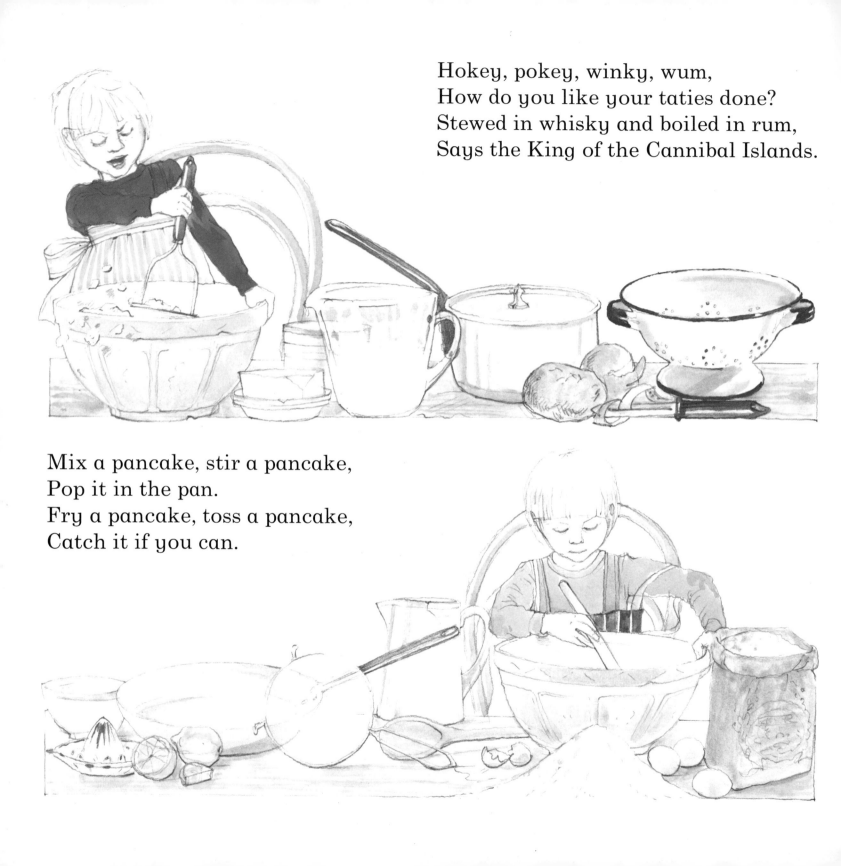

Hokey, pokey, winky, wum,
How do you like your taties done?
Stewed in whisky and boiled in rum,
Says the King of the Cannibal Islands.

Mix a pancake, stir a pancake,
Pop it in the pan.
Fry a pancake, toss a pancake,
Catch it if you can.

Manners in the dining room,
Manners in the hall.
If you don't behave yourself
You shan't have none at all.

Rain, rain, go away,
Come again another day;
All the children want to play,
So rain, rain, go away.

Stepping over stepping stones, one, two, three,
Stepping over stepping stones, come with me.
The river's very fast,
And the river's very wide,
And we'll step across on stepping stones
And reach the other side.

Miss Polly had a dolly who was sick, sick, sick,
So she phoned for the doctor to be quick, quick, quick.
The doctor came with her bag and her hat,
And she knocked on the door with a rat-a-tat-tat.

She looked at the dolly and she shook her head,
And she said, 'Miss Polly, put her straight to bed.'
She wrote on a paper for a pill, pill, pill,
'I'll be back in the morning with my bill, bill, bill.'

One-eyed Jack, the pirate chief,
Was a terrible, fearsome ocean thief.
He wore a peg
Upon one leg,
He wore a hook
And a dirty look,
One-eyed Jack, the pirate chief.

Dan, Dan,
Dirty old man,
Washed his face in a frying pan,
Combed his hair with the leg of a chair,
Dan, Dan,
Dirty old man.

1, 2, 3,
I give you a warning,
Do be better children
Before the morning!

Rigadoon, rigadoon,
Now let him fly,
Sit him on father's foot,
Jump him up high.

Father and Mother and Uncle John,
Went to market, one by one.
Father fell off!
Mother fell off!
But Uncle John went on and on,
And on, and on, and on.

I'm a little teapot,
Short and stout,
Here's my handle,
Here's my spout.
When I see the tea cups
I begin to shout,
'Tip me up, and pour me out.'

Little pig,
Pillimore,
Grimithistle,
Pennywhistle,
Great big Thumbo,
Father of them all.

Eye winker,
Tom thinker,
Nose smeller,
Mouth eater,
Chin chopper,
Guzzlewopper.

Go to bed late,
Stay very small.
Go to bed early,
Grow very tall.

Undo buttons,
Undo bows,
Skin a rabbit,
Off it goes.

Little man in a coal pit
Goes knock, knock, knock;
Up he comes, up he comes,
Out of the top.

One I love,
Two I love,
Three I love, I say;
Four I love with all my heart,
And shall do from this day.

Up the wooden hill
To Bedfordshire,
Down Sheet Lane
To Blanket Fair.

Niddledy, noddledy, to and fro,
Tired and sleepy, to bed we go.
Jump into bed,
Blow out the light,
Head on the pillow,
Shut your eyes tight.

Star light, star bright,
First star I see tonight,
I wish I may, I wish I might
Have the wish I wish tonight.